This Book Belongs To:

_____
_____
_____
_____

Copyright © 2021 by Collected Joys

All rights reserved. No part of this publication may be reproduced, distributed, or transmitted in any form without written permission from the author or publisher.

Congratulations on your new bundle of joy!

As a momma of two boys, I know how exciting yet overwhelming caring for a newborn can be. With sleepless nights and never-ending feedings and diapers, it can be hard to recall all the details of your baby's day. However, with this baby daily logbook, you can keep your newborn's schedules, activities, and needs all in one place to ensure your baby is happy and healthy!

Zady Rose
Collected Joys
www.collectedjoys.com

IMPORTANT CONTACTS

NAME	ADDRESS	PHONE
PEDIATRICIAN		
EMERGENCY ROOM		
HOSPITAL		
POISON CONTROL		
PHARMACY		

APPOINTMENT LOG

DOCTOR APPOINTMENTS

DATE	TIME	NOTES

QUESTIONS FOR THE DOCTOR & OTHER NOTES

H E A L T H   L O G

GROWTH LOG

DATE	WEIGHT	LENGTH	HEAD

IMMUNIZATIONS

DATE	NOTES

NOTES

SAMPLE BABY DAILY LOG

DATE	6/23/2021	AGE	3 weeks	WEIGHT	8 lbs. 6 oz.

FEEDINGS

BEGIN	END	SIDE		DURATION	BOTTLE oz/ml	PUMP oz/ml
8:15 am	8:23 am	(L)	R	8 min.		
8:24 am	8:30 am	L	(R)	6 min.		
10:30 am	10:45 am	L	R		4 oz	
		L	R			
		L	R			
		L	R			
		L	R			
		L	R			
		L	R			
		L	R			
		L	R			
		L	R			
		L	R			

Extra lines allow you to track breastfeeding, pumping, and bottle feedings. Record the total feeding time or record the duration for each breast separately.

NOTES

- Was a little fussy after morning bottle.

SAMPLE BABY DAILY LOG

ACTIVITIES

DESCRIPTION	DURATION
Tummy time	15 min.

DIAPER CHANGES

TIME	RESULT		COLOR
7:55 am	(WET)	BM	
9:52 am	WET	(BM)	B
	WET	BM	
	WET	BM	
	WET	BM	
	WET	BM	
	WET	BM	

> Track the time, result (wet or bowel movement), and color if necessary. In this example, we listed the first letter of the color for reference (B=Brown, G=Green, Y=Yellow).

MOOD

SLEEP / NAPS

START TIME	END TIME	DURATION	NOTES
2:00 am	6:00 am	4 hours	First 4 hour stretch!!
9:30 am	10:30 am	1 hour	

MEDICATIONS

TIME	NAME/DOSAGE
9:30 am	Vitamin D - 5ml

MEMORABLE MOMENTS/NOTES

- First smile today!
- Remember to buy diapers

BABY DAILY LOG

DATE		WEEK		WEIGHT	

FEEDINGS

BEGIN	END	SIDE		DURATION	BOTTLE oz/ml	PUMP oz/ml
		L	R			
		L	R			
		L	R			
		L	R			
		L	R			
		L	R			
		L	R			
		L	R			
		L	R			
		L	R			
		L	R			
		L	R			
		L	R			
		L	R			
		L	R			
		L	R			
		L	R			

NOTES

BABY DAILY LOG

ACTIVITIES

DESCRIPTION	DURATION

DIAPER CHANGES

TIME	RESULT		COLOR
	WET	BM	
	WET	BM	
	WET	BM	
	WET	BM	
	WET	BM	
	WET	BM	
	WET	BM	
	WET	BM	
	WET	BM	
	WET	BM	

MOOD

SLEEP / NAPS

START TIME	END TIME	DURATION	NOTES

MEDICATIONS

TIME	NAME/DOSAGE

MEMORABLE MOMENTS/NOTES

BABY DAILY LOG

DATE		WEEK		WEIGHT	

FEEDINGS

BEGIN	END	SIDE		DURATION	BOTTLE oz/ml	PUMP oz/ml
		L	R			
		L	R			
		L	R			
		L	R			
		L	R			
		L	R			
		L	R			
		L	R			
		L	R			
		L	R			
		L	R			
		L	R			
		L	R			
		L	R			
		L	R			
		L	R			
		L	R			
		L	R			

NOTES

BABY DAILY LOG

ACTIVITIES

DESCRIPTION	DURATION

MOOD

DIAPER CHANGES

TIME	RESULT		COLOR
	WET	BM	
	WET	BM	
	WET	BM	
	WET	BM	
	WET	BM	
	WET	BM	
	WET	BM	
	WET	BM	
	WET	BM	
	WET	BM	

SLEEP / NAPS

START TIME	END TIME	DURATION	NOTES

MEDICATIONS

TIME	NAME/DOSAGE

MEMORABLE MOMENTS/NOTES

BABY DAILY LOG

DATE		WEEK		WEIGHT	

FEEDINGS

BEGIN	END	SIDE		DURATION	BOTTLE oz/ml	PUMP oz/ml
		L	R			
		L	R			
		L	R			
		L	R			
		L	R			
		L	R			
		L	R			
		L	R			
		L	R			
		L	R			
		L	R			
		L	R			
		L	R			
		L	R			
		L	R			
		L	R			
		L	R			
		L	R			

NOTES

BABY DAILY LOG

ACTIVITIES	
DESCRIPTION	DURATION

DIAPER CHANGES			
TIME	RESULT		COLOR
	WET	BM	
	WET	BM	
	WET	BM	
	WET	BM	
	WET	BM	
	WET	BM	
	WET	BM	
	WET	BM	
	WET	BM	
	WET	BM	

MOOD

SLEEP / NAPS			
START TIME	END TIME	DURATION	NOTES

MEDICATIONS	
TIME	NAME/DOSAGE

MEMORABLE MOMENTS/NOTES

BABY DAILY LOG

DATE		WEEK		WEIGHT	

FEEDINGS

BEGIN	END	SIDE		DURATION	BOTTLE oz/ml	PUMP oz/ml
		L	R			
		L	R			
		L	R			
		L	R			
		L	R			
		L	R			
		L	R			
		L	R			
		L	R			
		L	R			
		L	R			
		L	R			
		L	R			
		L	R			
		L	R			
		L	R			
		L	R			
		L	R			

NOTES

BABY DAILY LOG

ACTIVITIES	
DESCRIPTION	DURATION

DIAPER CHANGES			
TIME	RESULT		COLOR
	WET	BM	
	WET	BM	
	WET	BM	
	WET	BM	
	WET	BM	
	WET	BM	
	WET	BM	
	WET	BM	
	WET	BM	
	WET	BM	

MOOD

SLEEP / NAPS			
START TIME	END TIME	DURATION	NOTES

MEDICATIONS	
TIME	NAME/DOSAGE

MEMORABLE MOMENTS/NOTES

BABY DAILY LOG

DATE		WEEK		WEIGHT	

FEEDINGS

BEGIN	END	SIDE		DURATION	BOTTLE oz/ml	PUMP oz/ml
		L	R			
		L	R			
		L	R			
		L	R			
		L	R			
		L	R			
		L	R			
		L	R			
		L	R			
		L	R			
		L	R			
		L	R			
		L	R			
		L	R			
		L	R			
		L	R			
		L	R			
		L	R			

NOTES

BABY DAILY LOG

ACTIVITIES

DESCRIPTION	DURATION

DIAPER CHANGES

TIME	RESULT		COLOR
	WET	BM	
	WET	BM	
	WET	BM	
	WET	BM	
	WET	BM	
	WET	BM	
	WET	BM	
	WET	BM	
	WET	BM	
	WET	BM	

MOOD

SLEEP / NAPS

START TIME	END TIME	DURATION	NOTES

MEDICATIONS

TIME	NAME/DOSAGE

MEMORABLE MOMENTS/NOTES

BABY DAILY LOG

DATE		WEEK		WEIGHT	

FEEDINGS

BEGIN	END	SIDE		DURATION	BOTTLE oz/ml	PUMP oz/ml
		L	R			
		L	R			
		L	R			
		L	R			
		L	R			
		L	R			
		L	R			
		L	R			
		L	R			
		L	R			
		L	R			
		L	R			
		L	R			
		L	R			
		L	R			
		L	R			
		L	R			
		L	R			

NOTES

BABY DAILY LOG

ACTIVITIES

DESCRIPTION	DURATION

DIAPER CHANGES

TIME	RESULT		COLOR
	WET	BM	
	WET	BM	
	WET	BM	
	WET	BM	
	WET	BM	
	WET	BM	
	WET	BM	
	WET	BM	
	WET	BM	
	WET	BM	

MOOD

SLEEP / NAPS

START TIME	END TIME	DURATION	NOTES

MEDICATIONS

TIME	NAME/DOSAGE

MEMORABLE MOMENTS/NOTES

BABY DAILY LOG

DATE		WEEK		WEIGHT	

FEEDINGS

BEGIN	END	SIDE		DURATION	BOTTLE oz/ml	PUMP oz/ml
		L	R			
		L	R			
		L	R			
		L	R			
		L	R			
		L	R			
		L	R			
		L	R			
		L	R			
		L	R			
		L	R			
		L	R			
		L	R			
		L	R			
		L	R			
		L	R			
		L	R			
		L	R			

NOTES

BABY DAILY LOG

ACTIVITIES

DESCRIPTION	DURATION

MOOD ☺ 😐 ☹

DIAPER CHANGES

TIME	RESULT		COLOR
	WET	BM	
	WET	BM	
	WET	BM	
	WET	BM	
	WET	BM	
	WET	BM	
	WET	BM	
	WET	BM	
	WET	BM	
	WET	BM	

SLEEP / NAPS

START TIME	END TIME	DURATION	NOTES

MEDICATIONS

TIME	NAME/DOSAGE

MEMORABLE MOMENTS/NOTES

BABY DAILY LOG

DATE		WEEK		WEIGHT	

FEEDINGS

BEGIN	END	SIDE		DURATION	BOTTLE oz/ml	PUMP oz/ml
		L	R			
		L	R			
		L	R			
		L	R			
		L	R			
		L	R			
		L	R			
		L	R			
		L	R			
		L	R			
		L	R			
		L	R			
		L	R			
		L	R			
		L	R			
		L	R			
		L	R			
		L	R			

NOTES

BABY DAILY LOG

ACTIVITIES

DESCRIPTION	DURATION

DIAPER CHANGES

TIME	RESULT		COLOR
	WET	BM	
	WET	BM	
	WET	BM	
	WET	BM	
	WET	BM	
	WET	BM	
	WET	BM	
	WET	BM	
	WET	BM	
	WET	BM	

MOOD

SLEEP / NAPS

START TIME	END TIME	DURATION	NOTES

MEDICATIONS

TIME	NAME/DOSAGE

MEMORABLE MOMENTS/NOTES

BABY DAILY LOG

DATE		WEEK		WEIGHT	

FEEDINGS

BEGIN	END	SIDE		DURATION	BOTTLE oz/ml	PUMP oz/ml
		L	R			
		L	R			
		L	R			
		L	R			
		L	R			
		L	R			
		L	R			
		L	R			
		L	R			
		L	R			
		L	R			
		L	R			
		L	R			
		L	R			
		L	R			
		L	R			
		L	R			
		L	R			

NOTES

BABY DAILY LOG

ACTIVITIES

DESCRIPTION	DURATION

DIAPER CHANGES

TIME	RESULT		COLOR
	WET	BM	
	WET	BM	
	WET	BM	
	WET	BM	
	WET	BM	
	WET	BM	
	WET	BM	
	WET	BM	
	WET	BM	
	WET	BM	

MOOD

SLEEP / NAPS

START TIME	END TIME	DURATION	NOTES

MEDICATIONS

TIME	NAME/DOSAGE

MEMORABLE MOMENTS/NOTES

BABY DAILY LOG

DATE		WEEK		WEIGHT	

FEEDINGS

BEGIN	END	SIDE		DURATION	BOTTLE oz/ml	PUMP oz/ml
		L	R			
		L	R			
		L	R			
		L	R			
		L	R			
		L	R			
		L	R			
		L	R			
		L	R			
		L	R			
		L	R			
		L	R			
		L	R			
		L	R			
		L	R			
		L	R			
		L	R			
		L	R			
		L	R			

NOTES

BABY DAILY LOG

ACTIVITIES

DESCRIPTION	DURATION

MOOD   ☹

DIAPER CHANGES

TIME	RESULT		COLOR
	WET	BM	
	WET	BM	
	WET	BM	
	WET	BM	
	WET	BM	
	WET	BM	
	WET	BM	
	WET	BM	
	WET	BM	
	WET	BM	

SLEEP / NAPS

START TIME	END TIME	DURATION	NOTES

MEDICATIONS

TIME	NAME/DOSAGE

MEMORABLE MOMENTS/NOTES

BABY DAILY LOG

DATE		WEEK		WEIGHT	

FEEDINGS						
BEGIN	END	SIDE		DURATION	BOTTLE oz/ml	PUMP oz/ml
		L	R			
		L	R			
		L	R			
		L	R			
		L	R			
		L	R			
		L	R			
		L	R			
		L	R			
		L	R			
		L	R			
		L	R			
		L	R			
		L	R			
		L	R			
		L	R			
		L	R			
		L	R			

NOTES

BABY DAILY LOG

ACTIVITIES

DESCRIPTION	DURATION

DIAPER CHANGES

TIME	RESULT		COLOR
	WET	BM	
	WET	BM	
	WET	BM	
	WET	BM	
	WET	BM	
	WET	BM	
	WET	BM	
	WET	BM	
	WET	BM	
	WET	BM	

MOOD

SLEEP / NAPS

START TIME	END TIME	DURATION	NOTES

MEDICATIONS

TIME	NAME/DOSAGE

MEMORABLE MOMENTS/NOTES

BABY DAILY LOG

DATE		WEEK		WEIGHT	

FEEDINGS

BEGIN	END	SIDE		DURATION	BOTTLE oz/ml	PUMP oz/ml
		L	R			
		L	R			
		L	R			
		L	R			
		L	R			
		L	R			
		L	R			
		L	R			
		L	R			
		L	R			
		L	R			
		L	R			
		L	R			
		L	R			
		L	R			
		L	R			
		L	R			

NOTES

BABY DAILY LOG

ACTIVITIES	
DESCRIPTION	DURATION

DIAPER CHANGES			
TIME	RESULT		COLOR
	WET	BM	
	WET	BM	
	WET	BM	
	WET	BM	
	WET	BM	
	WET	BM	
	WET	BM	
	WET	BM	
	WET	BM	
	WET	BM	

MOOD

SLEEP / NAPS			
START TIME	END TIME	DURATION	NOTES

MEDICATIONS	
TIME	NAME/DOSAGE

MEMORABLE MOMENTS/NOTES

BABY DAILY LOG

DATE		WEEK		WEIGHT	

FEEDINGS

BEGIN	END	SIDE		DURATION	BOTTLE oz/ml	PUMP oz/ml
		L	R			
		L	R			
		L	R			
		L	R			
		L	R			
		L	R			
		L	R			
		L	R			
		L	R			
		L	R			
		L	R			
		L	R			
		L	R			
		L	R			
		L	R			
		L	R			
		L	R			
		L	R			

NOTES

BABY DAILY LOG

ACTIVITIES	
DESCRIPTION	DURATION

MOOD

DIAPER CHANGES			
TIME	RESULT		COLOR
	WET	BM	
	WET	BM	
	WET	BM	
	WET	BM	
	WET	BM	
	WET	BM	
	WET	BM	
	WET	BM	
	WET	BM	
	WET	BM	

SLEEP / NAPS			
START TIME	END TIME	DURATION	NOTES

MEDICATIONS	
TIME	NAME/DOSAGE

MEMORABLE MOMENTS/NOTES

BABY DAILY LOG

DATE		WEEK		WEIGHT	

FEEDINGS

BEGIN	END	SIDE		DURATION	BOTTLE oz/ml	PUMP oz/ml
		L	R			
		L	R			
		L	R			
		L	R			
		L	R			
		L	R			
		L	R			
		L	R			
		L	R			
		L	R			
		L	R			
		L	R			
		L	R			
		L	R			
		L	R			
		L	R			
		L	R			
		L	R			

NOTES

BABY DAILY LOG

ACTIVITIES	
DESCRIPTION	DURATION

MOOD

DIAPER CHANGES			
TIME	RESULT		COLOR
	WET	BM	
	WET	BM	
	WET	BM	
	WET	BM	
	WET	BM	
	WET	BM	
	WET	BM	
	WET	BM	
	WET	BM	
	WET	BM	

SLEEP / NAPS			
START TIME	END TIME	DURATION	NOTES

MEDICATIONS	
TIME	NAME/DOSAGE

MEMORABLE MOMENTS/NOTES

BABY DAILY LOG

DATE		WEEK		WEIGHT	

FEEDINGS

BEGIN	END	SIDE		DURATION	BOTTLE oz/ml	PUMP oz/ml
		L	R			
		L	R			
		L	R			
		L	R			
		L	R			
		L	R			
		L	R			
		L	R			
		L	R			
		L	R			
		L	R			
		L	R			
		L	R			
		L	R			
		L	R			
		L	R			
		L	R			
		L	R			

NOTES

BABY DAILY LOG

ACTIVITIES	
DESCRIPTION	DURATION

DIAPER CHANGES			
TIME	RESULT		COLOR
	WET	BM	
	WET	BM	
	WET	BM	
	WET	BM	
	WET	BM	
	WET	BM	
	WET	BM	
	WET	BM	
	WET	BM	
	WET	BM	

MOOD

SLEEP / NAPS			
START TIME	END TIME	DURATION	NOTES

MEDICATIONS	
TIME	NAME/DOSAGE

MEMORABLE MOMENTS/NOTES

BABY DAILY LOG

| DATE | | WEEK | | WEIGHT | |

FEEDINGS

BEGIN	END	SIDE		DURATION	BOTTLE oz/ml	PUMP oz/ml
		L	R			
		L	R			
		L	R			
		L	R			
		L	R			
		L	R			
		L	R			
		L	R			
		L	R			
		L	R			
		L	R			
		L	R			
		L	R			
		L	R			
		L	R			
		L	R			
		L	R			
		L	R			

NOTES

BABY DAILY LOG

ACTIVITIES	
DESCRIPTION	DURATION

DIAPER CHANGES			
TIME	RESULT		COLOR
	WET	BM	
	WET	BM	
	WET	BM	
	WET	BM	
	WET	BM	
	WET	BM	
	WET	BM	
	WET	BM	
	WET	BM	
	WET	BM	

MOOD

SLEEP / NAPS			
START TIME	END TIME	DURATION	NOTES

MEDICATIONS	
TIME	NAME/DOSAGE

MEMORABLE MOMENTS/NOTES

BABY DAILY LOG

DATE		WEEK		WEIGHT	

FEEDINGS

BEGIN	END	SIDE		DURATION	BOTTLE oz/ml	PUMP oz/ml
		L	R			
		L	R			
		L	R			
		L	R			
		L	R			
		L	R			
		L	R			
		L	R			
		L	R			
		L	R			
		L	R			
		L	R			
		L	R			
		L	R			
		L	R			
		L	R			
		L	R			
		L	R			

NOTES

BABY DAILY LOG

ACTIVITIES

DESCRIPTION	DURATION

MOOD ☺ 😐 ☹

DIAPER CHANGES

TIME	RESULT		COLOR
	WET	BM	
	WET	BM	
	WET	BM	
	WET	BM	
	WET	BM	
	WET	BM	
	WET	BM	
	WET	BM	
	WET	BM	
	WET	BM	

SLEEP / NAPS

START TIME	END TIME	DURATION	NOTES

MEDICATIONS

TIME	NAME/DOSAGE

MEMORABLE MOMENTS/NOTES

BABY DAILY LOG

DATE		WEEK		WEIGHT	

FEEDINGS

BEGIN	END	SIDE		DURATION	BOTTLE oz/ml	PUMP oz/ml
		L	R			
		L	R			
		L	R			
		L	R			
		L	R			
		L	R			
		L	R			
		L	R			
		L	R			
		L	R			
		L	R			
		L	R			
		L	R			
		L	R			
		L	R			
		L	R			
		L	R			
		L	R			

NOTES

BABY DAILY LOG

ACTIVITIES

DESCRIPTION	DURATION

DIAPER CHANGES

TIME	RESULT		COLOR
	WET	BM	
	WET	BM	
	WET	BM	
	WET	BM	
	WET	BM	
	WET	BM	
	WET	BM	
	WET	BM	
	WET	BM	
	WET	BM	

MOOD

SLEEP / NAPS

START TIME	END TIME	DURATION	NOTES

MEDICATIONS

TIME	NAME/DOSAGE

MEMORABLE MOMENTS/NOTES

BABY DAILY LOG

DATE		WEEK		WEIGHT	

FEEDINGS

BEGIN	END	SIDE		DURATION	BOTTLE oz/ml	PUMP oz/ml
		L	R			
		L	R			
		L	R			
		L	R			
		L	R			
		L	R			
		L	R			
		L	R			
		L	R			
		L	R			
		L	R			
		L	R			
		L	R			
		L	R			
		L	R			
		L	R			
		L	R			
		L	R			

NOTES

BABY DAILY LOG

ACTIVITIES

DESCRIPTION	DURATION

DIAPER CHANGES

TIME	RESULT		COLOR
	WET	BM	
	WET	BM	
	WET	BM	
	WET	BM	
	WET	BM	
	WET	BM	
	WET	BM	
	WET	BM	
	WET	BM	
	WET	BM	

MOOD

SLEEP / NAPS

START TIME	END TIME	DURATION	NOTES

MEDICATIONS

TIME	NAME/DOSAGE

MEMORABLE MOMENTS/NOTES

BABY DAILY LOG

DATE		WEEK		WEIGHT	

FEEDINGS

BEGIN	END	SIDE		DURATION	BOTTLE oz/ml	PUMP oz/ml
		L	R			
		L	R			
		L	R			
		L	R			
		L	R			
		L	R			
		L	R			
		L	R			
		L	R			
		L	R			
		L	R			
		L	R			
		L	R			
		L	R			
		L	R			
		L	R			
		L	R			
		L	R			

NOTES

BABY DAILY LOG

ACTIVITIES

DESCRIPTION	DURATION

DIAPER CHANGES

TIME	RESULT		COLOR
	WET	BM	
	WET	BM	
	WET	BM	
	WET	BM	
	WET	BM	
	WET	BM	
	WET	BM	
	WET	BM	
	WET	BM	
	WET	BM	

MOOD

SLEEP / NAPS

START TIME	END TIME	DURATION	NOTES

MEDICATIONS

TIME	NAME/DOSAGE

MEMORABLE MOMENTS/NOTES

BABY DAILY LOG

DATE		WEEK		WEIGHT	

FEEDINGS

BEGIN	END	SIDE		DURATION	BOTTLE oz/ml	PUMP oz/ml
		L	R			
		L	R			
		L	R			
		L	R			
		L	R			
		L	R			
		L	R			
		L	R			
		L	R			
		L	R			
		L	R			
		L	R			
		L	R			
		L	R			
		L	R			
		L	R			
		L	R			
		L	R			

NOTES

BABY DAILY LOG

ACTIVITIES

DESCRIPTION	DURATION

MOOD ☺ 😐 ☹

DIAPER CHANGES

TIME	RESULT		COLOR
	WET	BM	
	WET	BM	
	WET	BM	
	WET	BM	
	WET	BM	
	WET	BM	
	WET	BM	
	WET	BM	
	WET	BM	
	WET	BM	

SLEEP / NAPS

START TIME	END TIME	DURATION	NOTES

MEDICATIONS

TIME	NAME/DOSAGE

MEMORABLE MOMENTS/NOTES

BABY DAILY LOG

DATE		WEEK		WEIGHT	

FEEDINGS

BEGIN	END	SIDE		DURATION	BOTTLE oz/ml	PUMP oz/ml
		L	R			
		L	R			
		L	R			
		L	R			
		L	R			
		L	R			
		L	R			
		L	R			
		L	R			
		L	R			
		L	R			
		L	R			
		L	R			
		L	R			
		L	R			
		L	R			
		L	R			
		L	R			

NOTES

BABY DAILY LOG

ACTIVITIES

DESCRIPTION	DURATION

DIAPER CHANGES

TIME	RESULT		COLOR
	WET	BM	
	WET	BM	
	WET	BM	
	WET	BM	
	WET	BM	
	WET	BM	
	WET	BM	
	WET	BM	
	WET	BM	
	WET	BM	

MOOD

SLEEP / NAPS

START TIME	END TIME	DURATION	NOTES

MEDICATIONS

TIME	NAME/DOSAGE

MEMORABLE MOMENTS/NOTES

BABY DAILY LOG

DATE		WEEK		WEIGHT	

FEEDINGS

BEGIN	END	SIDE		DURATION	BOTTLE oz/ml	PUMP oz/ml
		L	R			
		L	R			
		L	R			
		L	R			
		L	R			
		L	R			
		L	R			
		L	R			
		L	R			
		L	R			
		L	R			
		L	R			
		L	R			
		L	R			
		L	R			
		L	R			
		L	R			
		L	R			

NOTES

BABY DAILY LOG

ACTIVITIES

DESCRIPTION	DURATION

MOOD

DIAPER CHANGES

TIME	RESULT		COLOR
	WET	BM	
	WET	BM	
	WET	BM	
	WET	BM	
	WET	BM	
	WET	BM	
	WET	BM	
	WET	BM	
	WET	BM	
	WET	BM	

SLEEP / NAPS

START TIME	END TIME	DURATION	NOTES

MEDICATIONS

TIME	NAME/DOSAGE

MEMORABLE MOMENTS/NOTES

BABY DAILY LOG

DATE		WEEK		WEIGHT	

FEEDINGS

BEGIN	END	SIDE		DURATION	BOTTLE oz/ml	PUMP oz/ml
		L	R			
		L	R			
		L	R			
		L	R			
		L	R			
		L	R			
		L	R			
		L	R			
		L	R			
		L	R			
		L	R			
		L	R			
		L	R			
		L	R			
		L	R			
		L	R			
		L	R			
		L	R			

NOTES

BABY DAILY LOG

ACTIVITIES

DESCRIPTION	DURATION

DIAPER CHANGES

TIME	RESULT		COLOR
	WET	BM	
	WET	BM	
	WET	BM	
	WET	BM	
	WET	BM	
	WET	BM	
	WET	BM	
	WET	BM	
	WET	BM	
	WET	BM	

MOOD

SLEEP / NAPS

START TIME	END TIME	DURATION	NOTES

MEDICATIONS

TIME	NAME/DOSAGE

MEMORABLE MOMENTS/NOTES

BABY DAILY LOG

DATE		WEEK		WEIGHT	

FEEDINGS

BEGIN	END	SIDE		DURATION	BOTTLE oz/ml	PUMP oz/ml
		L	R			
		L	R			
		L	R			
		L	R			
		L	R			
		L	R			
		L	R			
		L	R			
		L	R			
		L	R			
		L	R			
		L	R			
		L	R			
		L	R			
		L	R			
		L	R			
		L	R			
		L	R			

NOTES

BABY DAILY LOG

ACTIVITIES	
DESCRIPTION	DURATION

DIAPER CHANGES			
TIME	RESULT		COLOR
	WET	BM	
	WET	BM	
	WET	BM	
	WET	BM	
	WET	BM	
	WET	BM	
	WET	BM	
	WET	BM	
	WET	BM	
	WET	BM	

MOOD

SLEEP / NAPS			
START TIME	END TIME	DURATION	NOTES

MEDICATIONS	
TIME	NAME/DOSAGE

MEMORABLE MOMENTS/NOTES

BABY DAILY LOG

DATE		WEEK		WEIGHT	

FEEDINGS

BEGIN	END	SIDE		DURATION	BOTTLE oz/ml	PUMP oz/ml
		L	R			
		L	R			
		L	R			
		L	R			
		L	R			
		L	R			
		L	R			
		L	R			
		L	R			
		L	R			
		L	R			
		L	R			
		L	R			
		L	R			
		L	R			
		L	R			
		L	R			
		L	R			

NOTES

BABY DAILY LOG

ACTIVITIES	
DESCRIPTION	DURATION

DIAPER CHANGES			
TIME	RESULT		COLOR
	WET	BM	
	WET	BM	
	WET	BM	
	WET	BM	
	WET	BM	
	WET	BM	
	WET	BM	
	WET	BM	
	WET	BM	
	WET	BM	

MOOD

SLEEP / NAPS			
START TIME	END TIME	DURATION	NOTES

MEDICATIONS	
TIME	NAME/DOSAGE

MEMORABLE MOMENTS/NOTES

BABY DAILY LOG

DATE		WEEK		WEIGHT	

FEEDINGS

BEGIN	END	SIDE		DURATION	BOTTLE oz/ml	PUMP oz/ml
		L	R			
		L	R			
		L	R			
		L	R			
		L	R			
		L	R			
		L	R			
		L	R			
		L	R			
		L	R			
		L	R			
		L	R			
		L	R			
		L	R			
		L	R			
		L	R			
		L	R			
		L	R			

NOTES

BABY DAILY LOG

ACTIVITIES

DESCRIPTION	DURATION

MOOD ☺ 😐 ☹

DIAPER CHANGES

TIME	RESULT		COLOR
	WET	BM	
	WET	BM	
	WET	BM	
	WET	BM	
	WET	BM	
	WET	BM	
	WET	BM	
	WET	BM	
	WET	BM	
	WET	BM	

SLEEP / NAPS

START TIME	END TIME	DURATION	NOTES

MEDICATIONS

TIME	NAME/DOSAGE

MEMORABLE MOMENTS/NOTES

BABY DAILY LOG

DATE		WEEK		WEIGHT	

FEEDINGS

BEGIN	END	SIDE		DURATION	BOTTLE oz/ml	PUMP oz/ml
		L	R			
		L	R			
		L	R			
		L	R			
		L	R			
		L	R			
		L	R			
		L	R			
		L	R			
		L	R			
		L	R			
		L	R			
		L	R			
		L	R			
		L	R			
		L	R			
		L	R			
		L	R			

NOTES

BABY DAILY LOG

ACTIVITIES

DESCRIPTION	DURATION

MOOD ☺ 😐 ☹

DIAPER CHANGES

TIME	RESULT		COLOR
	WET	BM	
	WET	BM	
	WET	BM	
	WET	BM	
	WET	BM	
	WET	BM	
	WET	BM	
	WET	BM	
	WET	BM	
	WET	BM	

SLEEP / NAPS

START TIME	END TIME	DURATION	NOTES

MEDICATIONS

TIME	NAME/DOSAGE

MEMORABLE MOMENTS/NOTES

BABY DAILY LOG

DATE		WEEK		WEIGHT	

FEEDINGS

BEGIN	END	SIDE		DURATION	BOTTLE oz/ml	PUMP oz/ml
		L	R			
		L	R			
		L	R			
		L	R			
		L	R			
		L	R			
		L	R			
		L	R			
		L	R			
		L	R			
		L	R			
		L	R			
		L	R			
		L	R			
		L	R			
		L	R			
		L	R			
		L	R			

NOTES

BABY DAILY LOG

ACTIVITIES	
DESCRIPTION	DURATION

DIAPER CHANGES			
TIME	RESULT		COLOR
	WET	BM	
	WET	BM	
	WET	BM	
	WET	BM	
	WET	BM	
	WET	BM	
	WET	BM	
	WET	BM	
	WET	BM	
	WET	BM	

MOOD

SLEEP / NAPS			
START TIME	END TIME	DURATION	NOTES

MEDICATIONS	
TIME	NAME/DOSAGE

MEMORABLE MOMENTS/NOTES

BABY DAILY LOG

DATE		WEEK		WEIGHT	

FEEDINGS

BEGIN	END	SIDE		DURATION	BOTTLE oz/ml	PUMP oz/ml
		L	R			
		L	R			
		L	R			
		L	R			
		L	R			
		L	R			
		L	R			
		L	R			
		L	R			
		L	R			
		L	R			
		L	R			
		L	R			
		L	R			
		L	R			
		L	R			
		L	R			
		L	R			

NOTES

BABY DAILY LOG

ACTIVITIES

DESCRIPTION	DURATION

DIAPER CHANGES

TIME	RESULT		COLOR
	WET	BM	
	WET	BM	
	WET	BM	
	WET	BM	
	WET	BM	
	WET	BM	
	WET	BM	
	WET	BM	
	WET	BM	
	WET	BM	

MOOD

SLEEP / NAPS

START TIME	END TIME	DURATION	NOTES

MEDICATIONS

TIME	NAME/DOSAGE

MEMORABLE MOMENTS/NOTES

BABY DAILY LOG

DATE		WEEK		WEIGHT	

FEEDINGS

BEGIN	END	SIDE		DURATION	BOTTLE oz/ml	PUMP oz/ml
		L	R			
		L	R			
		L	R			
		L	R			
		L	R			
		L	R			
		L	R			
		L	R			
		L	R			
		L	R			
		L	R			
		L	R			
		L	R			
		L	R			
		L	R			
		L	R			
		L	R			
		L	R			

NOTES

BABY DAILY LOG

ACTIVITIES

DESCRIPTION	DURATION

MOOD ☺ ☺ ☹

DIAPER CHANGES

TIME	RESULT		COLOR
	WET	BM	
	WET	BM	
	WET	BM	
	WET	BM	
	WET	BM	
	WET	BM	
	WET	BM	
	WET	BM	
	WET	BM	
	WET	BM	

SLEEP / NAPS

START TIME	END TIME	DURATION	NOTES

MEDICATIONS

TIME	NAME/DOSAGE

MEMORABLE MOMENTS/NOTES

BABY DAILY LOG

DATE		WEEK		WEIGHT	

FEEDINGS

BEGIN	END	SIDE		DURATION	BOTTLE oz/ml	PUMP oz/ml
		L	R			
		L	R			
		L	R			
		L	R			
		L	R			
		L	R			
		L	R			
		L	R			
		L	R			
		L	R			
		L	R			
		L	R			
		L	R			
		L	R			
		L	R			
		L	R			
		L	R			
		L	R			
		L	R			

NOTES

BABY DAILY LOG

ACTIVITIES

DESCRIPTION	DURATION

MOOD   ☺   😐   ☹

DIAPER CHANGES

TIME	RESULT		COLOR
	WET	BM	
	WET	BM	
	WET	BM	
	WET	BM	
	WET	BM	
	WET	BM	
	WET	BM	
	WET	BM	
	WET	BM	
	WET	BM	

SLEEP / NAPS

START TIME	END TIME	DURATION	NOTES

MEDICATIONS

TIME	NAME/DOSAGE

MEMORABLE MOMENTS/NOTES

BABY DAILY LOG

DATE		WEEK		WEIGHT	

FEEDINGS

BEGIN	END	SIDE		DURATION	BOTTLE oz/ml	PUMP oz/ml
		L	R			
		L	R			
		L	R			
		L	R			
		L	R			
		L	R			
		L	R			
		L	R			
		L	R			
		L	R			
		L	R			
		L	R			
		L	R			
		L	R			
		L	R			
		L	R			
		L	R			
		L	R			

NOTES

BABY DAILY LOG

ACTIVITIES

DESCRIPTION	DURATION

DIAPER CHANGES

TIME	RESULT		COLOR
	WET	BM	
	WET	BM	
	WET	BM	
	WET	BM	
	WET	BM	
	WET	BM	
	WET	BM	
	WET	BM	
	WET	BM	
	WET	BM	

MOOD

SLEEP / NAPS

START TIME	END TIME	DURATION	NOTES

MEDICATIONS

TIME	NAME/DOSAGE

MEMORABLE MOMENTS/NOTES

BABY DAILY LOG

DATE		WEEK		WEIGHT	

FEEDINGS

BEGIN	END	SIDE		DURATION	BOTTLE oz/ml	PUMP oz/ml
		L	R			
		L	R			
		L	R			
		L	R			
		L	R			
		L	R			
		L	R			
		L	R			
		L	R			
		L	R			
		L	R			
		L	R			
		L	R			
		L	R			
		L	R			
		L	R			
		L	R			
		L	R			
		L	R			

NOTES

BABY DAILY LOG

ACTIVITIES

DESCRIPTION	DURATION

DIAPER CHANGES

TIME	RESULT		COLOR
	WET	BM	
	WET	BM	
	WET	BM	
	WET	BM	
	WET	BM	
	WET	BM	
	WET	BM	
	WET	BM	
	WET	BM	
	WET	BM	

MOOD

SLEEP / NAPS

START TIME	END TIME	DURATION	NOTES

MEDICATIONS

TIME	NAME/DOSAGE

MEMORABLE MOMENTS/NOTES

BABY DAILY LOG

DATE		WEEK		WEIGHT	

FEEDINGS

BEGIN	END	SIDE		DURATION	BOTTLE oz/ml	PUMP oz/ml
		L	R			
		L	R			
		L	R			
		L	R			
		L	R			
		L	R			
		L	R			
		L	R			
		L	R			
		L	R			
		L	R			
		L	R			
		L	R			
		L	R			
		L	R			
		L	R			
		L	R			
		L	R			

NOTES

BABY DAILY LOG

ACTIVITIES

DESCRIPTION	DURATION

MOOD ☺ 😐 ☹

DIAPER CHANGES

TIME	RESULT		COLOR
	WET	BM	
	WET	BM	
	WET	BM	
	WET	BM	
	WET	BM	
	WET	BM	
	WET	BM	
	WET	BM	
	WET	BM	
	WET	BM	

SLEEP / NAPS

START TIME	END TIME	DURATION	NOTES

MEDICATIONS

TIME	NAME/DOSAGE

MEMORABLE MOMENTS/NOTES

BABY DAILY LOG

DATE		WEEK		WEIGHT	

FEEDINGS

BEGIN	END	SIDE		DURATION	BOTTLE oz/ml	PUMP oz/ml
		L	R			
		L	R			
		L	R			
		L	R			
		L	R			
		L	R			
		L	R			
		L	R			
		L	R			
		L	R			
		L	R			
		L	R			
		L	R			
		L	R			
		L	R			
		L	R			
		L	R			
		L	R			

NOTES

BABY DAILY LOG

ACTIVITIES

DESCRIPTION	DURATION

DIAPER CHANGES

TIME	RESULT		COLOR
	WET	BM	
	WET	BM	
	WET	BM	
	WET	BM	
	WET	BM	
	WET	BM	
	WET	BM	
	WET	BM	
	WET	BM	
	WET	BM	

MOOD

SLEEP / NAPS

START TIME	END TIME	DURATION	NOTES

MEDICATIONS

TIME	NAME/DOSAGE

MEMORABLE MOMENTS/NOTES

BABY DAILY LOG

DATE		WEEK		WEIGHT	

FEEDINGS

BEGIN	END	SIDE		DURATION	BOTTLE oz/ml	PUMP oz/ml
		L	R			
		L	R			
		L	R			
		L	R			
		L	R			
		L	R			
		L	R			
		L	R			
		L	R			
		L	R			
		L	R			
		L	R			
		L	R			
		L	R			
		L	R			
		L	R			
		L	R			
		L	R			

NOTES

BABY DAILY LOG

ACTIVITIES	
DESCRIPTION	DURATION

DIAPER CHANGES			
TIME	RESULT		COLOR
	WET	BM	
	WET	BM	
	WET	BM	
	WET	BM	
	WET	BM	
	WET	BM	
	WET	BM	
	WET	BM	
	WET	BM	
	WET	BM	

MOOD

SLEEP / NAPS			
START TIME	END TIME	DURATION	NOTES

MEDICATIONS	
TIME	NAME/DOSAGE

MEMORABLE MOMENTS/NOTES

BABY DAILY LOG

DATE		WEEK		WEIGHT	

FEEDINGS

BEGIN	END	SIDE		DURATION	BOTTLE oz/ml	PUMP oz/ml
		L	R			
		L	R			
		L	R			
		L	R			
		L	R			
		L	R			
		L	R			
		L	R			
		L	R			
		L	R			
		L	R			
		L	R			
		L	R			
		L	R			
		L	R			
		L	R			
		L	R			
		L	R			

NOTES

BABY DAILY LOG

ACTIVITIES

DESCRIPTION	DURATION

DIAPER CHANGES

TIME	RESULT		COLOR
	WET	BM	
	WET	BM	
	WET	BM	
	WET	BM	
	WET	BM	
	WET	BM	
	WET	BM	
	WET	BM	
	WET	BM	
	WET	BM	

MOOD

SLEEP / NAPS

START TIME	END TIME	DURATION	NOTES

MEDICATIONS

TIME	NAME/DOSAGE

MEMORABLE MOMENTS/NOTES

BABY DAILY LOG

DATE		WEEK		WEIGHT	

FEEDINGS

BEGIN	END	SIDE		DURATION	BOTTLE oz/ml	PUMP oz/ml
		L	R			
		L	R			
		L	R			
		L	R			
		L	R			
		L	R			
		L	R			
		L	R			
		L	R			
		L	R			
		L	R			
		L	R			
		L	R			
		L	R			
		L	R			
		L	R			
		L	R			
		L	R			

NOTES

BABY DAILY LOG

ACTIVITIES

DESCRIPTION	DURATION

DIAPER CHANGES

TIME	RESULT		COLOR
	WET	BM	
	WET	BM	
	WET	BM	
	WET	BM	
	WET	BM	
	WET	BM	
	WET	BM	
	WET	BM	
	WET	BM	
	WET	BM	

MOOD

SLEEP / NAPS

START TIME	END TIME	DURATION	NOTES

MEDICATIONS

TIME	NAME/DOSAGE

MEMORABLE MOMENTS/NOTES

BABY DAILY LOG

DATE		WEEK		WEIGHT	

FEEDINGS

BEGIN	END	SIDE		DURATION	BOTTLE oz/ml	PUMP oz/ml
		L	R			
		L	R			
		L	R			
		L	R			
		L	R			
		L	R			
		L	R			
		L	R			
		L	R			
		L	R			
		L	R			
		L	R			
		L	R			
		L	R			
		L	R			
		L	R			
		L	R			
		L	R			

NOTES

BABY DAILY LOG

ACTIVITIES	
DESCRIPTION	DURATION

MOOD

DIAPER CHANGES			
TIME	RESULT		COLOR
	WET	BM	
	WET	BM	
	WET	BM	
	WET	BM	
	WET	BM	
	WET	BM	
	WET	BM	
	WET	BM	
	WET	BM	
	WET	BM	

SLEEP / NAPS			
START TIME	END TIME	DURATION	NOTES

MEDICATIONS	
TIME	NAME/DOSAGE

MEMORABLE MOMENTS/NOTES

BABY DAILY LOG

DATE		WEEK		WEIGHT	

FEEDINGS

BEGIN	END	SIDE		DURATION	BOTTLE oz/ml	PUMP oz/ml
		L	R			
		L	R			
		L	R			
		L	R			
		L	R			
		L	R			
		L	R			
		L	R			
		L	R			
		L	R			
		L	R			
		L	R			
		L	R			
		L	R			
		L	R			
		L	R			
		L	R			
		L	R			

NOTES

BABY DAILY LOG

ACTIVITIES	
DESCRIPTION	DURATION

MOOD

DIAPER CHANGES			
TIME	RESULT		COLOR
	WET	BM	
	WET	BM	
	WET	BM	
	WET	BM	
	WET	BM	
	WET	BM	
	WET	BM	
	WET	BM	
	WET	BM	
	WET	BM	

SLEEP / NAPS			
START TIME	END TIME	DURATION	NOTES

MEDICATIONS	
TIME	NAME/DOSAGE

MEMORABLE MOMENTS/NOTES

BABY DAILY LOG

DATE		WEEK		WEIGHT	

FEEDINGS

BEGIN	END	SIDE		DURATION	BOTTLE oz/ml	PUMP oz/ml
		L	R			
		L	R			
		L	R			
		L	R			
		L	R			
		L	R			
		L	R			
		L	R			
		L	R			
		L	R			
		L	R			
		L	R			
		L	R			
		L	R			
		L	R			
		L	R			
		L	R			
		L	R			

NOTES

BABY DAILY LOG

ACTIVITIES

DESCRIPTION	DURATION

DIAPER CHANGES

TIME	RESULT		COLOR
	WET	BM	
	WET	BM	
	WET	BM	
	WET	BM	
	WET	BM	
	WET	BM	
	WET	BM	
	WET	BM	
	WET	BM	
	WET	BM	

MOOD

SLEEP / NAPS

START TIME	END TIME	DURATION	NOTES

MEDICATIONS

TIME	NAME/DOSAGE

MEMORABLE MOMENTS/NOTES

BABY DAILY LOG

DATE		WEEK		WEIGHT	

FEEDINGS

BEGIN	END	SIDE		DURATION	BOTTLE oz/ml	PUMP oz/ml
		L	R			
		L	R			
		L	R			
		L	R			
		L	R			
		L	R			
		L	R			
		L	R			
		L	R			
		L	R			
		L	R			
		L	R			
		L	R			
		L	R			
		L	R			
		L	R			
		L	R			
		L	R			

NOTES

BABY DAILY LOG

ACTIVITIES	
DESCRIPTION	DURATION

DIAPER CHANGES			
TIME	RESULT		COLOR
	WET	BM	
	WET	BM	
	WET	BM	
	WET	BM	
	WET	BM	
	WET	BM	
	WET	BM	
	WET	BM	
	WET	BM	
	WET	BM	

MOOD

SLEEP / NAPS			
START TIME	END TIME	DURATION	NOTES

MEDICATIONS	
TIME	NAME/DOSAGE

MEMORABLE MOMENTS/NOTES

BABY DAILY LOG

DATE		WEEK		WEIGHT	

FEEDINGS

BEGIN	END	SIDE		DURATION	BOTTLE oz/ml	PUMP oz/ml
		L	R			
		L	R			
		L	R			
		L	R			
		L	R			
		L	R			
		L	R			
		L	R			
		L	R			
		L	R			
		L	R			
		L	R			
		L	R			
		L	R			
		L	R			
		L	R			
		L	R			
		L	R			

NOTES

BABY DAILY LOG

ACTIVITIES	
DESCRIPTION	DURATION

DIAPER CHANGES			
TIME	RESULT		COLOR
	WET	BM	
	WET	BM	
	WET	BM	
	WET	BM	
	WET	BM	
	WET	BM	
	WET	BM	
	WET	BM	
	WET	BM	
	WET	BM	

MOOD

SLEEP / NAPS			
START TIME	END TIME	DURATION	NOTES

MEDICATIONS	
TIME	NAME/DOSAGE

MEMORABLE MOMENTS/NOTES

BABY DAILY LOG

DATE		WEEK		WEIGHT	

FEEDINGS

BEGIN	END	SIDE		DURATION	BOTTLE oz/ml	PUMP oz/ml
		L	R			
		L	R			
		L	R			
		L	R			
		L	R			
		L	R			
		L	R			
		L	R			
		L	R			
		L	R			
		L	R			
		L	R			
		L	R			
		L	R			
		L	R			
		L	R			
		L	R			
		L	R			

NOTES

BABY DAILY LOG

ACTIVITIES

DESCRIPTION	DURATION

MOOD ☺ 😐 ☹

DIAPER CHANGES

TIME	RESULT		COLOR
	WET	BM	
	WET	BM	
	WET	BM	
	WET	BM	
	WET	BM	
	WET	BM	
	WET	BM	
	WET	BM	
	WET	BM	
	WET	BM	

SLEEP / NAPS

START TIME	END TIME	DURATION	NOTES

MEDICATIONS

TIME	NAME/DOSAGE

MEMORABLE MOMENTS/NOTES

BABY DAILY LOG

DATE		WEEK		WEIGHT	

FEEDINGS

BEGIN	END	SIDE		DURATION	BOTTLE oz/ml	PUMP oz/ml
		L	R			
		L	R			
		L	R			
		L	R			
		L	R			
		L	R			
		L	R			
		L	R			
		L	R			
		L	R			
		L	R			
		L	R			
		L	R			
		L	R			
		L	R			
		L	R			
		L	R			
		L	R			

NOTES

BABY DAILY LOG

ACTIVITIES

DESCRIPTION	DURATION

MOOD ☺ 😐 ☹

DIAPER CHANGES

TIME	RESULT		COLOR
	WET	BM	
	WET	BM	
	WET	BM	
	WET	BM	
	WET	BM	
	WET	BM	
	WET	BM	
	WET	BM	
	WET	BM	
	WET	BM	

SLEEP / NAPS

START TIME	END TIME	DURATION	NOTES

MEDICATIONS

TIME	NAME/DOSAGE

MEMORABLE MOMENTS/NOTES

BABY DAILY LOG

DATE		WEEK		WEIGHT	

FEEDINGS

BEGIN	END	SIDE		DURATION	BOTTLE oz/ml	PUMP oz/ml
		L	R			
		L	R			
		L	R			
		L	R			
		L	R			
		L	R			
		L	R			
		L	R			
		L	R			
		L	R			
		L	R			
		L	R			
		L	R			
		L	R			
		L	R			
		L	R			
		L	R			
		L	R			

NOTES

BABY DAILY LOG

ACTIVITIES

DESCRIPTION	DURATION

DIAPER CHANGES

TIME	RESULT		COLOR
	WET	BM	
	WET	BM	
	WET	BM	
	WET	BM	
	WET	BM	
	WET	BM	
	WET	BM	
	WET	BM	
	WET	BM	
	WET	BM	

MOOD

SLEEP / NAPS

START TIME	END TIME	DURATION	NOTES

MEDICATIONS

TIME	NAME/DOSAGE

MEMORABLE MOMENTS/NOTES

BABY DAILY LOG

DATE		WEEK		WEIGHT	

FEEDINGS

BEGIN	END	SIDE		DURATION	BOTTLE oz/ml	PUMP oz/ml
		L	R			
		L	R			
		L	R			
		L	R			
		L	R			
		L	R			
		L	R			
		L	R			
		L	R			
		L	R			
		L	R			
		L	R			
		L	R			
		L	R			
		L	R			
		L	R			
		L	R			
		L	R			

NOTES

BABY DAILY LOG

ACTIVITIES

DESCRIPTION	DURATION

DIAPER CHANGES

TIME	RESULT		COLOR
	WET	BM	
	WET	BM	
	WET	BM	
	WET	BM	
	WET	BM	
	WET	BM	
	WET	BM	
	WET	BM	
	WET	BM	
	WET	BM	

MOOD

SLEEP / NAPS

START TIME	END TIME	DURATION	NOTES

MEDICATIONS

TIME	NAME/DOSAGE

MEMORABLE MOMENTS/NOTES

BABY DAILY LOG

DATE		WEEK		WEIGHT	

FEEDINGS

BEGIN	END	SIDE		DURATION	BOTTLE oz/ml	PUMP oz/ml
		L	R			
		L	R			
		L	R			
		L	R			
		L	R			
		L	R			
		L	R			
		L	R			
		L	R			
		L	R			
		L	R			
		L	R			
		L	R			
		L	R			
		L	R			
		L	R			
		L	R			
		L	R			

NOTES

BABY DAILY LOG

ACTIVITIES

DESCRIPTION	DURATION

DIAPER CHANGES

TIME	RESULT		COLOR
	WET	BM	
	WET	BM	
	WET	BM	
	WET	BM	
	WET	BM	
	WET	BM	
	WET	BM	
	WET	BM	
	WET	BM	
	WET	BM	

MOOD

SLEEP / NAPS

START TIME	END TIME	DURATION	NOTES

MEDICATIONS

TIME	NAME/DOSAGE

MEMORABLE MOMENTS/NOTES

BABY DAILY LOG

DATE		WEEK		WEIGHT	

FEEDINGS

BEGIN	END	SIDE		DURATION	BOTTLE oz/ml	PUMP oz/ml
		L	R			
		L	R			
		L	R			
		L	R			
		L	R			
		L	R			
		L	R			
		L	R			
		L	R			
		L	R			
		L	R			
		L	R			
		L	R			
		L	R			
		L	R			
		L	R			
		L	R			
		L	R			

NOTES

BABY DAILY LOG

ACTIVITIES

DESCRIPTION	DURATION

MOOD ☺ 😐 ☹

DIAPER CHANGES

TIME	RESULT		COLOR
	WET	BM	
	WET	BM	
	WET	BM	
	WET	BM	
	WET	BM	
	WET	BM	
	WET	BM	
	WET	BM	
	WET	BM	
	WET	BM	

SLEEP / NAPS

START TIME	END TIME	DURATION	NOTES

MEDICATIONS

TIME	NAME/DOSAGE

MEMORABLE MOMENTS/NOTES

BABY DAILY LOG

DATE		WEEK		WEIGHT	

FEEDINGS

BEGIN	END	SIDE		DURATION	BOTTLE oz/ml	PUMP oz/ml
		L	R			
		L	R			
		L	R			
		L	R			
		L	R			
		L	R			
		L	R			
		L	R			
		L	R			
		L	R			
		L	R			
		L	R			
		L	R			
		L	R			
		L	R			
		L	R			
		L	R			
		L	R			

NOTES

BABY DAILY LOG

ACTIVITIES

DESCRIPTION	DURATION

MOOD ☺ 😐 ☹

DIAPER CHANGES

TIME	RESULT		COLOR
	WET	BM	
	WET	BM	
	WET	BM	
	WET	BM	
	WET	BM	
	WET	BM	
	WET	BM	
	WET	BM	
	WET	BM	
	WET	BM	

SLEEP / NAPS

START TIME	END TIME	DURATION	NOTES

MEDICATIONS

TIME	NAME/DOSAGE

MEMORABLE MOMENTS/NOTES

BABY DAILY LOG

DATE		WEEK		WEIGHT	

FEEDINGS

BEGIN	END	SIDE		DURATION	BOTTLE oz/ml	PUMP oz/ml
		L	R			
		L	R			
		L	R			
		L	R			
		L	R			
		L	R			
		L	R			
		L	R			
		L	R			
		L	R			
		L	R			
		L	R			
		L	R			
		L	R			
		L	R			
		L	R			
		L	R			
		L	R			

NOTES

BABY DAILY LOG

ACTIVITIES

DESCRIPTION	DURATION

DIAPER CHANGES

TIME	RESULT		COLOR
	WET	BM	
	WET	BM	
	WET	BM	
	WET	BM	
	WET	BM	
	WET	BM	
	WET	BM	
	WET	BM	
	WET	BM	
	WET	BM	

MOOD

SLEEP / NAPS

START TIME	END TIME	DURATION	NOTES

MEDICATIONS

TIME	NAME/DOSAGE

MEMORABLE MOMENTS/NOTES

BABY DAILY LOG

DATE		WEEK		WEIGHT	

FEEDINGS

BEGIN	END	SIDE		DURATION	BOTTLE oz/ml	PUMP oz/ml
		L	R			
		L	R			
		L	R			
		L	R			
		L	R			
		L	R			
		L	R			
		L	R			
		L	R			
		L	R			
		L	R			
		L	R			
		L	R			
		L	R			
		L	R			
		L	R			
		L	R			
		L	R			

NOTES

BABY DAILY LOG

ACTIVITIES

DESCRIPTION	DURATION

DIAPER CHANGES

TIME	RESULT		COLOR
	WET	BM	
	WET	BM	
	WET	BM	
	WET	BM	
	WET	BM	
	WET	BM	
	WET	BM	
	WET	BM	
	WET	BM	
	WET	BM	

MOOD

SLEEP / NAPS

START TIME	END TIME	DURATION	NOTES

MEDICATIONS

TIME	NAME/DOSAGE

MEMORABLE MOMENTS/NOTES

BABY DAILY LOG

DATE		WEEK		WEIGHT	

FEEDINGS

BEGIN	END	SIDE		DURATION	BOTTLE oz/ml	PUMP oz/ml
		L	R			
		L	R			
		L	R			
		L	R			
		L	R			
		L	R			
		L	R			
		L	R			
		L	R			
		L	R			
		L	R			
		L	R			
		L	R			
		L	R			
		L	R			
		L	R			
		L	R			
		L	R			

NOTES

BABY DAILY LOG

ACTIVITIES

DESCRIPTION	DURATION

DIAPER CHANGES

TIME	RESULT		COLOR
	WET	BM	
	WET	BM	
	WET	BM	
	WET	BM	
	WET	BM	
	WET	BM	
	WET	BM	
	WET	BM	
	WET	BM	
	WET	BM	

MOOD

SLEEP / NAPS

START TIME	END TIME	DURATION	NOTES

MEDICATIONS

TIME	NAME/DOSAGE

MEMORABLE MOMENTS/NOTES

NOTES

NOTES

NOTES

NOTES

NOTES

Printed in Great Britain
by Amazon

48091262R00069